KIMONO
with Young Girl Sleeves

Available from Box Turtle Press, Inc.

184 Franklin Street
New York, New York 10013
212.219.9278; mudfishmag@aol.com
www.mudfish.org

ISBN: 978-1-893654-34-1

Front Cover: "Kimono with Young Girl Sleeves," (detail)
2022, Jill Hoffman, oil on canvas, 30"x40"
Back Cover: "Kimono with Young Girl Sleeves"

Book Design: Anne Lawrence
Typeset in Futura Book

Copyright @2024 Jill Hoffman
Publisher: Box Turtule Press, Inc.
Box Turtle Press, Inc. is a 501(c)(3) not-for-profit organization.

All rights reserved

KIMONO
with Young Girl Sleeves

Poems
Jill Hoffman

For
Stephanie Emily Dickinson

TABLE OF CONTENTS

	PAGE
Reading Michael Fried	1
Aubade	4
I am Carlos, I will Scan your Heart	6
Jenny Kissed Me	8
John Singer Sargent	9
Thanks to Coronavirus	10
Snake Arms	12
Oh, My Dear Franz	14
Thou Preparest a Table Before Me	16
Light Years	17
Mirage	19
Sonnet for John Ashbery	20
On the Table	21
A Dog Is Where We Put Our Soul	22
Messaging	23
I Am Young	24
Becoming Pearl	25
Lost Poem	26
Dog Sorrow	27
O My America	28
Watching the News	29
In Front of Issey Miyake	30
Late August, Franklin Street	33
Damaged Area	35
Staggering	36
Moulin Bleu	38
Hard to Talk	39

	PAGE
Croissants	40
A Frank Stella	41
And Summer's Lease Hath All Too Short a Date	42
Death Mask	43
Duane Reade	44
A Resemblance	45
The Brothers Krents	46
I Must Clean the House, A Guest Is Coming	47
Lines In Search of a Villanelle	48
Gürtlerose	49
Odyssey	50
Vladimir	51
Vermeer	53
Liens	55
Mausoleum	56
Judge Wanted	57
John Ashbery Celebration on Zoom	59
A Serpent's Tooth	60
A Fine Confusion	61
Ghosts	62
Saab	63
Knee Replacement	65
Death and the Maiden	67
Kimono with Young Girl Sleeves	68
The Mascara Brush	69
Lame Villanelle	70
In July, Death Comes to Franklin Street	71

	PAGE
Still Life	72
Divorce	73
Older Women	75
Hand-Painted Scenes	77
Jane Campion	80
My Kimono	82
The Contract	84
Jenny	85
Butter Knives	86
Relay	87
Adam	88
A Bushel and a Peck	89
A Russian Fairytale	91
Different Line Breaks	92
Weekend Getaway	94
Marvin	95
His Painting	97
They Who One Another Keep Alive	98
Past Life	99
Hello, Barry	100
You Need a Book	101
Ittai Weinryb	102
Bambu Paper	103
Bad Flowers	104
Speech After Silence	107
Ellipsis	108
Falling	109

	PAGE
Red Dot	110
Old Couple	111
Instagram	112
For Joyce	113
Jenny, Again	114
George Segal	116
Golan Heights	117
Surrounded By Friends Waving Hamas Flags	119
Dancing On Our Own Graves	120
If Only To Go Warm Were Gorgeous	121
Hard Work	122
Before and After	123
The Rape Tree	124
What If This Present Were the World's Last Night?	126

READING MICHAEL FRIED

He was my first love.
He went to Oxford on a Rhodes
Scholarship and met two
Sisters. Twins, I think.
He was supposed to marry
One but he married the other.
"I was walking through London
With a friend, late at night, very
Full of myself, and saw her sitting
On a stoop, sobbing," he told me.
I think about poor Jean Rhys.
Jean Rhys fell in love with an
Aristocrat who knew the King.
He dumped her and never married.
She got so skinny she fell
Into a toilet and the young man
Who rescued her from her
Solitude one day for a drive
In the country had to
Pull her out. Michael Fried is
In love with painting
(Manet's *Déjeuner sur l'herbe*)
Though he doesn't paint.
He was asked at a panel
Discussion, "What is your biggest

Regret?" "That my poems aren't
Recognized," he said. Then he
Added, "But they will be
In a thousand years." I was there.
He didn't recognize me.
"I want to be the lover
Not the lovee," he said.
He taught me to write. *Jill*
Hoffman agrees with me
When I attack her poems. Now
She must write good poems!
I sent him Special Delivery
Letters in Cambridge one winter.
He complained the postman
Shouted up the stairs, Fried,
Fried, like eggs over lightly,
Like my brain is fried
From smoking grass. My lips
Purse. I look in the mirror.
Mother, I say to the first face.
Daddy, I say to another.
The black line from the tip
Of my lips on the right
Side to the droop of my cheek
And chin, as if in black
Paint an inch thick, is my
Celebration of long life —

Or a portrait by Rouault.
I bought his third book
Years ago. (The first I memorized.)
He railed against sunglasses
Boasting, "I didn't wear them
Even in Italy." But on the glossy
Back cover are large black shades
Covering his narrow eyes.
Like the ungenerous peasant woman
Who kept baking pies in *A Child's
History of England*, each too
Good for King Alfred in disguise,
He is transformed Into a
Blackbird that caws of passion.

AUBADE

Say I was in the camps
And my friends were all gone
And walking around me
   as memories
In their grey striped pyjamas

Not lying in the Bay of Skeletons
   anymore, naked

And my dog was licking my cunt

And Felix Nussbaum was painting
   barbed wire
Like a necklace of lace
With a few prisoners penned in,
   one shitting on a tall can

And I was in love with him
But couldn't show it because he
   was dead

And I was saved by reciting poetry
   in my head
But only until morning

When the trees would relinquish
    darkness, barefoot

And you said I was trivializing
    the Holocaust
As you scrubbed on hands and
    knees
In your striped seersucker robe

I AM CARLOS, I WILL SCAN YOUR HEART

I cried when Gladys
texted in Spanish asking
God to spare her for
one more year *si Dios
me permite* when I
needed her to vacuum
and help me clean
the pantry. She had a
knee replacement at
Bellevue and nearly
died from infection and
still can't walk a year
later.
     I will walk the
plank tomorrow to the
department of electro
physiology at Mt. Sinai
Beth Israel to have a
ticking clock implanted
in my chest. The hospital
workers in masks are all
there waiting in Dazian
eleventh floor. Like Captain
Hook I am thrown
overboard, like we all
are.

Gone is my girlhood
my mermaid breasts. Gone
my mother, my father,
Terry, Abby, friends,
poets, men, three
dogs I loved; the one
on my lap looks up at me
with concern in his onyx
eyes as I keen my song
of telemetry. Goodbye,
goodbye, we are not here
for long.

JENNY KISSED ME

Say I'm weary, say I'm sad,
Say that health, and wealth, have missed me,
Say I'm growing old, but add
Jenny kissed me.
                              Leigh Hunt

I saw my daughter shovel dirt into my grave.
I was far down deep in the ground
— green tarps over large mounds of earth —
wearing my green Chinese robe in the coffin
with the hole in the silk lining that Vermeer had dug
who gnaws bright marrow bone around his paw
and isn't allowed in the cemetery. Her face
was wet with tears. Her long salt and pepper hair
smooth as if she had just been to Drybar
but she hadn't had it done for ten days.
She held the heavy shovel upside down
with difficulty balancing the trickling dirt
that slid off before the reverberant thud
— like angry banging on the ceiling if my TV was too loud —
to show that she didn't want to bid farewell
and bury me efficiently, and in fact I didn't want to go —
I wanted to lie naked with my arms around your body
under the silk-velvet and polyester quilt
and have hot flashes all night long and make coffee
in the morning and eat raisin and walnut bread
on the painted plates that Alice had given us
and stop Vermeer from eating books
but what made my heart spill over
was how beautiful she looked.

JOHN SINGER SARGENT

I want to paint like Bonnard, like Vuillard, like Munch.
Mica visits who used to be Micael. She is huge,
tall, in a black one shoulder halter with a bare midriff.
Red lipstick, red nail polish, a man's black umbrella
and rain boots. Long skinny legs under a black skirt, bald
with earrings. Her necklace is simple, like a key chain.
I forgot that he had a heavy accent from Brazil
or Israel. I fell in love with him long ago
at a book party when he was wearing a grey silk
blouse that I admired without noticing anything
strange. I think he had a beard then. When I looked
into his eyes I saw the essence of intelligence.
My mind dilated. He was Plato and Tiresias.
Now I remember that I loved him.
                                    At dinner I make
a big mistake. I tell the waitress, Linda, "*He's* not eating."
"She," he corrects me, "I'm a girl." "Do you have a lot of
boyfriends?" I ask to make amends. He has just gotten
a divorce from Pedro. "No! Friendship is more important
than love," he answers. "My three ex-wives are my best friends.
I enjoy sex with men but I have always been more comfortable
with women. I am happy," he says. "You can see that."
His new belly button is round and deep. "Nietzsche
said something very wise," he says. "Love is blind,
but friendship closes its eyes." He has opened my
eyes. I longed to paint her. But I never did.

THANKS TO CORONAVIRUS

I stay in, rapt among
paintings
jeweling the walls
of this mausoleum

The past catches up with me

Chinese food every Sunday
night in Forest Hills — I had no idea
Chinks was racist

or that Wuhan would
ruin the world

Thanks to Coronavirus
Lawrence, my photographer,
is busy digging up
old photos he sends me –

grandchildren in
tiny sizes,
Sammy the Frenchie
adorable in his black and
white design

and there I am
in my old younger skin,
my hair before chemo
curled it
Now it is grey
under dark sheets

Thanks to Coronavirus
I see my daughter on the screen
Her red lips,
the twist of her mouth
when she talks

which reminds me of her
infant yawn,
a trace of silver in her hair

Zoom has given me her face

SNAKE ARMS

Mermaids everywhere. Hanging from the tree
in the garden; combing their hair under my Mac.
One in the backyard sitting on a rock
with a realistic fishnet tail. "It's all right except for
the breasts," my crazy sister said,
whose gift it had been the year before.
I feed the dog from a chipped mermaid plate.
My friend who whelped him is Dutch
so we named him Vermeer—it means, 'from the sea,'
Van der Meer, but we have trouble saying it.
My grandson Shepherd calls him Root Beer.
The last time my son visited he said I was too old
to get a dog. The minute he went home
to Georgia he and his wife decided on a breed.
Their Labradoodle was in doggy day care every
weekend so his wife wouldn't have to deal with it.
"She won't have anything to do with the dog,"
he told my daughter. "The children wanted one."
New York never looked better than when my son
arrived Pride weekend with two of his children.
I was Wendy in Never-Never-Land.
First the playground, then breakfast at Sarabeth's
where the boy was punished for hitting the girl.
"*She* hit *me*," Parker said and I saw my daughter

nod her head yes. "No I didn't," his sister said.
Still the boy punched and kicked his father
in the groin, and butted him with his head
even at the Natural History Museum and Central
Park where Parker fell into the Turtle Pond.
Before they left, we went on a half-hour ferry trip
so they could see the Statue of Liberty, sold out
till September and aloof in her tarnished drapery.
"What was your best moment in New York?"
their father asked. "I know what my worst
moment was," Parker volunteered.
I ran out on the street to say goodbye to them.
Uber was there. "Come back," I cried politely
as their luggage was loaded into the trunk
but, like the maimed mermaid who had her tongue
cut out, I could not say the word, "Soon!"
In belly dancing I forget I am not a mermaid.
My two legs bent at the knee become one,
my arms are seaweed snaking in the depths
to rescue a lost boy from pirate turtles.

OH, MY DEAR FRANZ

On my Guggenheim
On Sundays
In London
(Our first day there
A brick nearly fell
On my husband's head),
At bus stops
With my two adoring
Young children
And him
(We were writing *Joint Novel*
Together),
With my incredibly
Bad voice, I sang,
–*Oh, is he dead?*
Well, there's no more to be said.
Lustily, loudly,
I belted it out,
Oh, is he ill?
Well, give him a pill.
Waiting for the triumphant
Bus of my infidelity
To arrive like Cleopatra's
Barge and carry me

Back to Antony
On Jones Street
In Greenwich Village.
At the end of the year
—Woman, go home,
His Will's to be read—
I crossed the adulterous ocean
And over the phone
In his raspy voice,
"I'm engaged," he said.

THOU PREPAREST A TABLE BEFORE ME

My old funny life
Of heartbreak
And ecstasy
I think back on
Fondly, how he loved
My best friend
Terry de Antonio
Who was dying
Of leukemia, but I thought
He loved me
Even after she told me
The truth, confessing
If you knew how he wooed me...

And you agree
That you can love two women
At once, But you say, with solemnity,
I know one thing: No man has ever
loved you as much as I love you,
While we are having morning coffee
At the near end of our lives
And tears well
Like my grandmother Bella's
Who Mrs. Matheis the maid said
Would cry when she had to
Get up
From the table.

LIGHT YEARS

I remember the arrogance
Of my unmade bed.
My student Marjorie and I sat
On the edge of it.
She gave me a paperback novel
I didn't read for decades.

        In that book
James Salter wrote about anal
Intercourse.

        The girl in the kitchen
Greasing herself with chicken fat,
Climbing the stairs. He put silver
Pieces on her back. She had
Married. *Something wrong
At home?* he asked. *No,
'Jes habit,* she said. The narrator
Says she was his real "wife."
I am on my knees with her,
Feeling her pleasure.

        You will be buried
Next to the one who wore
Your last name embroidered
On her apron.

        Once in London
When I went for a bikini wax

The aproned woman told me
My hair was put on backwards.
My body like a book in Hebrew,
The first page is the last.
You knead my hips, my ass,
You turn the mysterious pages.

MIRAGE

Leaving Whole Foods
On Greenwich Street
Magnolias and tulips
Hold out their cups
For shedding tears
Or viruses, bananas
Hanging out the top
Over boxes of matzos
Like Jews escaping
You in your copper

Jacket coming towards me
In the far distance to help
Pull the wagon home
A mirage, an orange
Sunlit pole—only blocks
Later emerging from benches
And trees in your white
Mask and dark fleece
Sweater
Like a Vuillard

SONNET FOR JOHN ASHBERY

With a grotesque fear that you may not be
as humble
as you seem, I see the Sycophant
approach. There is a
blare.
She has blown her own trumpet.
Again.
And in the background sit the king and
queen
of your gentleness and grandeur
doing something hand-in-hand
as on the page
more convex and anonymous I hope than passing
judgment.

ON THE TABLE

The dog coughs, quacks like a duck
or sneezes as we take his walk. Bless you,
someone says. Others smile.

His heart is enlarged, his bronchi trailing off
in the wrong direction. I see his little stomach
filled with black air in the x-ray.

                                      He is on the metal table
and the room is too bright yellow for me to hear
the Greek Vet speak in her white gown. She has a

dog herself who coughs. A Brittany Spaniel. "You remembered,"
she says. Then Jack calls, stuck in traffic.
                                    "Jack is on the table," I cry

to him. He had been on the table recently, operated on.
Now under his left collar bone there is a shelf
for me to lay my head on.

She prescribes two pills day and night: codeine and
theophylline. I force one tablet down his throat, but the capsule
slides out of his jaw repeatedly. He forgives me

and climbs coughing on to Jack's pillow on my bed.
The next day, I buy London Broil thinly sliced at the deli
counter, fragrant and limp. I enfold each pill

in a fragment of beef like the dual defibrillator
and pacemaker enthroned in my lover's chest.

He is eager, and eats.

A DOG IS WHERE WE PUT OUR SOUL

(Lesle Lewis, *Small Boats*)

My soul is under the bed
dying.
He hasn't eaten for six days.
He follows me from room to room
like the white shadow
he has always been, buoying me
with his devotion.
A Japanese Chin
who has stepped out of a painting,
a few orange leaves
scattered on his body.
Everyone is sorry.
He is a lesson in mortality.
We are all dying.
Especially we
who are losing him.
He lies down on the sidewalk
as if he wants to die outside.
It is Indian Summer.
I will fly like Wendy
to sew him to me with white thread.

MESSAGING

My heart is texting:
I go out on the street
with a Whole Foods wagon
that I pulled Obi in
when he couldn't walk
on his last trip
to the Vet. He recoiled
only once for a split
second when they came
for him in the waiting room.
Instead of begging
he avoided us when we ate.
When the Vet said his numbers
were off the chart, I thought
the chart must be wrong.
He wasn't eleven yet.
I am 80 and my heart
presses send.

I AM YOUNG

My own hair friends me.
Every month on Friday
my dyed eyebrows
are two young girls
on my forehead. Belly
dancing my arms, thin
from the elbow down,
wrinkle and I am at a
loss to understand it.
My legs in bed
wrap around you like
a monkey and we marvel
at your erection
without Viagra or Cialis
lasting even after you
cramp, agonizingly,
and stand up in
profile, testicles
like pompoms or
drooping pink roses.

BECOMING PEARL

My daughter calls.
"We are all becoming Pearl,"
she says. Her dog kept
motionless in a wire playpen
after a spinal operation.
"I have to ask
Andy to rotate my legs in the
morning." The dog named
after my mother.
                   But my dog, my dog
died, I realize
as I hang up the phone,
remembering that I woke in the night
because he had to pee and went into
the pantry and opened the door to
let him out into the backyard
and saw that he wasn't there behind
me, that he didn't have to pee
and I walked back alone
down the long hall howling
while he drank from his bowl
in the kitchen and hearing my
howls sound his death knell
he turned and glancing at me
once walked quietly
back to his cave
under my bed.

LOST POEM

In the bathroom sink, I remove
a dingleberry, grab a towel,
hold the tiny puppy against me
soaking my Chinese emerald robe,
and sit with him on my lap
at the computer reconstituting
my new lost poem.

When I saw a shrink I always
dreamt about clogged toilets.
It was my own unpublished
writing, we figured out.

Then on the Mac screen
it was there suddenly
like a lost twin in a Shakespeare
play, washed up on the shore,
auto-recovered
like a dream, but even better
than I remembered.

DOG SORROW

I think of the black and grey poodles.
The man who owned them appeared one day
with only one. "The black dog
taught him everything he knew." The grey dog
that had always been so friendly
wouldn't look at me.

Then I think of Obi after Barclay died
in gorgeous weather refusing to go out.
They used to tear out of the house at dawn together.

But the worst, the very worst
was when we went to a computer guy
in Connecticut and Obi
alone in the backseat all the way there
bounded up the steps
of the strange house, ran inside

searching the rooms
and not finding Barclay
lay down
quietly
at my feet
not saying a word.

O MY AMERICA

George Floyd on the cross, Macy's
is burning
Small businesses in my
neighborhood
reduced to uncut diamonds strewn
on sidewalks

The word *looting* forbidden

Walking the dog after curfew
past walls of plywood
like the cheapest coffin you can buy
Suffocating in a camouflage
designer mask

The man I never knew
turns over in my privileged heart
calling for
our mother

WATCHING THE NEWS

Hands clasped—fingers lying on
top of one another like bodies
of the dead—ten down
in a mass shooting—

This is what we are good at.

IN FRONT OF ISSEY MIYAKE

where he used to sit with his dog,
he called out to us and then rose.
Who are you? I said, unable to see
in the glare of the streetlight and
the lit window behind him. We were
walking our dog; it was sad not to
see him with his. Where is Georgia?
I asked, remembering her name.
A chocolate lab who had visited once
and passing our door always pulled
to come in. "She's with my wife. For
the past fifteen months they're always
together. Even in the bathroom.
They're like this," and he put two
fingers together, like my new legs
after knee replacement surgery,
straight and touching one another.
"I left home," he said. "I'm going to
sleep here." There was a stone
bed behind him with a cloth bookbag,
his pillow. Then his story streamed forth
like a show on Netflix, seasons of episodes
that hook you into long nights of binge-
watching. "'Why did you put your
cigarette on the table?' she said, and

then it went to my shoes on the floor.
'Where am I going to put them,' I said,
'we live in two rooms'?" I could see it,
like a building pancaking in Florida.
My son has just bought a house in Georgia
with a swimming pool so the three children
will like him better than his wife. Everyone
is divorcing. Jack's son told him he was in
'enormous pain' but when Jack tried to help
he called it 'nosiness.' "Don't get mad,"
Jack said. "And don't move out. A lawyer
told me that. It's called 'abandonment.'
Just go home and plan an exit strategy."
Our friend pulled a few homeless bills
from his pocket. One dollar for the advice
not to get mad, another for the advice
not to move out, but a big five for Jack's advice
to go home and plan an exit strategy.
"It's not that I get mad," he said,
"it's more that I got tired of batting away
her abuse." I showed him the long scar
on my knee that let me walk again.
"Look at *me* walk," he said. and
staggered like a villain in a horror movie.

He was joking, I thought at first. The next day
at 8:00 a.m. when Jack went to sit in the car
for alternate side parking, he wasn't there.
He had gone home, we thought, or to a hotel.
Then, three evenings later, from our car window,
a group of three, walking contentedly on
Greenwich Street, a woman, a dog, and a man
in a billowing white Issey Miyake shirt were unrecognizable
at dusk, except for the man's Frankenstein gait.

LATE AUGUST, FRANKLIN STREET

The sun forgets how cold it is—
bears down like mid-summer while
the air is full of Fall outfits and pencil
sharpeners. Whales are plunging on
the Cape and the tiny house in North
Truro with its crossed oars and
peeling porch overlooking the ocean's
blue gauze immensity
is padlocked and carted away.

Summers ago, her
amber necklace hanging from a
hook my mother said would walk
—That necklace will walk, she said.
The fragile door unlocked.
I smoked pot all day.
We sent the children off
to find other children, the girl
holding her little brother's hand.
A boy from the lighthouse
humiliating her: I saw your mother
naked, he said. Naked, my body
greased with olive oil, we picked
blackberries and ate the wild tangle
of the hills, while I dreamed of the

subway that would take me to his
bed. Maybe it will work out for us
when we're old, he said.

And coming back once I met my
father, my face ravaged with
pleasure that I thought had no stop
or station. Why do you look so sad?
he asked prophetically, my free lawyer
for the divorce before he died
and left me to find out the reason.
Skin wrinkling like low tide,
my body forgets how old it is
and basks in sunset every morning.

DAMAGED AREA

See, this is the
damaged area, they told me
in the hospital.
My brain on its stem
a white dandelion
like the white Pomeranian
on my lap
that I can't walk
because I can't walk
even from chair to chair
after a stroke
           Once
I was the little mermaid
who trod the marble palace floors
where every step was a knife
Now I am the little octopus
with my many arms
holding on
to dear life.

STAGGERING

Yellow leaves from Klimt
tile the sidewalks.
I stop every few steps
and think about my left knee
which needs replacement.
Almost home I see Mike,
whose father died yesterday
in Guyana, at the top of the stairs
to the basement studio he is painting
and vacuuming with an industrial vacuum,
so I can rent it.

It was a love nest.

After 14 years my beloved tenant
Kazushi
and his partner Rieko flew back to Japan
because in Japan there is only
one death a day.

I was in tears
above my red satin mask that spells SECRET
in large white sparkly teeth.

Stephanie Emily

Dickinson whose yellow hair blows from a kitchen fan
on Zoom, whose brown eyes loom, a fleeing deer
wearing heels from Payless and antlers
of immortal books, said:

No way out

but the Grand Exit,

but this staggering

                    November night after pitiless

     rain is like my dying mother's poem

I ridiculed,

         "I Will Stay Longer at the Fair."

MOULIN BLEU

for Adelle

The year begins
like a grave opening.
Old days of dissatisfaction
precious now. Your lovesick
dog Truffles slobbering on
Obi, you and Bob standing in the
street looking at the commercial
space you would fill with antiques
from Italy before his stroke
and Alzheimers. You moved
to what had been a brothel
in Oregon when he died. Got married
and divorced in seconds.
We lost track of each other.
My thigh-high boots excruciating
before a double bypass.
The velvet striped chairs, the
vintage leather couch,
the chandelier in my bedroom
—we live in a brothel of borrowed
treasure. Obi's cocked face on my
iphone, dark mauve triangle
of nose and mouth, sorrowful
eyes always there
under the date and time
every third minute
when I check for mail.

HARD TO TALK

My daughter called me after two weeks.
I had fantasized she was dead, a distant
memory. Or I was dead, and she was
living on, going about her business
without me. Then I heard her upbeat
voice again clear as a bell. She had been
to a very sad funeral all day for an old
woman whom she claimed was young,
still teaching celebrities, who was
shoved hailing a cab, and died. I had
seen her on TV at the piano, I said.
Then funny gossip framed like a painting
of a young person we both knew "so old
and ugly" she said, "it was hard to talk to her,"
while we avoided all mention of politics
and I rose from my grave like Lazarus.

CROISSANTS

The tree wearing mermaid earrings
at breakfast on the deck, the arm of
a woman in the Greenwich Hotel dusting
windows in the sky, fire escapes, air
conditioners, shadows of leaves

on the white brick wall,
I think of Felix Nussbaum
and the watery soup with
dirt thrown in
that was served to Jews.

A FRANK STELLA

Last night I dreamed that I was robbed.
My computer was gone from my desk.

A Frank Stella, the day before, was missing
from the wall. I had forgotten to tell you.

It slipped my mind. Someone had slipped in
from the front door or the back

and taken it. It was my fault, I knew. I left the doors
open. I tried to call the police in the dream

but loud voices were everywhere. I woke up;
the TV was on. I am my own shrink: it was you

who had slipped in from the front door
and the back. Nothing was backed up.

I had lost everything. But I was open again.
I left myself open and you backed in.

AND SUMMER'S LEASE HATH ALL TOO SHORT A DATE

My mother's portrait safe under the overhang,
I sit on the back stoop in the downpour
to watch the rain erase the white splotches
on the deck. The owl motionless on a post
wards off the pigeons, except for a brazen
pair or two, its beak sharp as the future.
One dead rhododendron bush an eyesore,
toxic leaves curdled into a bronze heap, the other
green and shiny. The Japanese maple turned redhead
on an upper branch, its slender trunk long and bare
like Maria Tall Chief; the mermaid whetting her tail
and breasts. A cemetery in Eden. Soon it will belong
to someone else. The dog a flower from my own garden
I will wear to my funeral like Frida Kahlo.

DEATH MASK

Asleep in the Eames chair mouth
open
black laptop open beneath
your clasped hands,
the black night a tomb
into which we all must inevitably
tumble

Failed implants, failed work
product, failed bank account and
parenting,
I wake up each morning happy
my five loose teeth are still there

DUANE READE

O do not die for I will hate
all days and nights
when you are gone

The dog will freeze
at the door
waiting
for your return

arms full
with coffee and toilet
paper

A RESEMBLANCE

Coal black eyes
Pink belly with brown testicles

Our love dog loves love
But not criticism
I am the same

I will cut off your balls in your sleep, I claim

THE BROTHERS KRENTS

I'm Jasper, I have curls, he told
strangers. I publish his early
drawing that says, *Speak now
or forever hold your
penis.* Skateboarding,
he breaks his ankle. A drummer,
he breaks his drumstick.
Draws constantly.

Shepherd paints like Hans
Hoffmann. Later, a hunk, he
waits in suspense
to see if he's made the ice
hockey team—he texts me
the coach (that he spells
couch) called him aside
and said, you have
hockey sense.

During Covid they grew up
and when I saw them on the
couch in their sunken
living room
and then only one,
I said, Jasper, where's Shepherd?
I *am* Shepherd, Shepherd says.

I MUST CLEAN THE HOUSE, A GUEST IS COMING

She will open the drawers
of my negligence

She will unearth the keys in the urn
for nights I was locked out
with my little dog

She will dismantle the wardrobe of
my days and toss the designer
masks in which I could hardly
breathe

And empty the sewing basket from
my mother with its decrepit spools
and don the gold coral-tipped
thimble
to give me the finger

As I lie in the grave with a tarnished
silver hand-mirror
and my latest book of poems

She will snoop like my daughter and
find the long
pulled incisor with a gold crown

The half-eaten placenta and
umbilical cord

LINES IN SEARCH OF A VILLANELLE

My life is on the scales on my father's desk
that the bronze lady who is blindfolded holds.
She is blindfolded and I am blindfolded.

And my father isn't here to sit across from
or phone. I see him sitting in cars
and then I blink and he's gone.

Christmas his car (his precious golf clubs
in the trunk) was stolen on my block
and then his heart attack broke our hearts.

He walks on my grave a welcome ghost
and a friend to my wishes that nobody knows.
I blow out the candle on a miniature cake
and the waitress brings a handful of spoons.

GÜRTLEROSE

A cottage with red
shingles

Inside, a witch
stirs
the devil's
darning needles
in a cauldron of ribs

ODYSSEY

For five years after she died
Donald Hall told me
Jane Kenyon's dog, Gus,
Couldn't figure out
Where she'd gone.
Vermeer and I
Go to Whole Foods
With the shopping cart
For a last-minute dinner
And while I search
For 90% lean beef, organic
Raspberries, and anything
Else on sale, he turns in
Circles in every aisle, shopping
Frantically for your jeans,
Your shoes, your hands,
Your smell.

VLADIMIR

Moving furniture
I found an old photograph
slightly curled, glossy
from three decades ago
a piece of time
next to some mouse droppings

you in a plaid flannel shirt
in a bar, without me
talking earnestly to a floozie
in a baseball cap
(she was wearing a strapless
top despite huge arms)
who was also talking
her mouth open

and you were holding
hands

And I remember the photograph
on a high shelf
that fluttered to the floor
in the bedroom once
this same woman
that you had tucked up there
thinking I would never see it

and your refusal to let me tear up
any bad photo of me
that I hated because for you
every photo
was sacred

Every woman was after you
and I didn't mind
that you never got a job
because you might meet someone
at work

Then the dresser was carried
out and the small desk
and the empty drawers one by
one
The sad thing was
not that I thought you were faithful
all those years, but
in a second bent
photo of us on a strange couch

how young I was
smiling and vibrant
in my orange and purple
pineapple
skirt

VERMEER

His white tail
a Monet haystack
a lady's bustle
a fur muff I had when I was four
not only the dog
but the furniture, the paintings on the walls,
the worn carpets, the used candles
draped in minute ruffles around the bronze
rim of two candlesticks, the scant red tulips
on the glass table
all like shining pebbles
still wet from the sea
everything seen as if for the last time
the first time
like a scene from "Our Town" with dead people
in the wings looking on
matzoh crumbs at our feet

or watching the third season of
"Shtisel" at night
on Netflix, transported
to Israel under a velvet quilt
the rapid subtitles invisible against white
Orthodox garments
almost unnecessary in the clarity
of life

you open the door to leave
and then return
—I sit holding him—
to kiss me, like touching
the mezuzah

LIENS

I brush white fur off dark gaucho
pants waiting for you
in the parking lot of Stop & Shop
I write on my cell phone:
The dog leaned against me in the night
The pigeon leans his weight on
another pigeon on the low store roof
The clouds lean their grey bellies
on the blue supine sky—
while coyotes lurk, salivating
in the dappled wood—I heard one
snatched the leash from a woman's
hand and ran off with her dog while
she watched—and the IRS
just down the road and across the street
from the Motor Vehicle Bureau
in Bloomsbury, Connecticut, leans
on your house

MAUSOLEUM

When I came across the word 'insulation'
as I read, that pink insulation where we lay
in his immense studio, his mausoleum,
that he tore out of his own half-built walls
after we climbed the ladder to our bower
to cushion us in a cone of cotton candy
while his helpers sauntered below

made me perch still married and young
in tall Dior boots and tight jeans on the top
rung earthshaking moments or months
before the dim future's cathedral ceiling
collapsed on me, tearing the pith out of
the stiff walls of my heart, turning
my entire insides into a pink volcano

JUDGE WANTED

Dear Marie Howe, I first saw two
poems of yours in *The New Yorker*
and was swept away. Will you be
the next judge of the Mudfish Poetry
Prize?

      I have run out of living poets
to ask.

      Dear John Crowe Ransom,
I love your poetry. Will you be
the next judge of the Mudfish
Poetry Prize (I once promised
John Ashbery an apple pie
as payment but never delivered)?
Dear William Empson, your
villanelles are among the most
cherished poems I've memorized.
I was surprised and delighted to hear
John Ashbery say at a reading in Soho
once that you were underappreciated.
Will you be the judge of the next
Mudfish Poetry Prize? No, for
reasons you cannot explain, you won't.
Dear W.H. Auden, John Ashbery
invited me to a dinner with you

at the Gotham Book Mart when I was
nine months pregnant. Keep me away
from pregnant women you wrote.
I dare not ask you to be a judge.
What if the winner was great with child?
The grave's a fine and private place
but no one there wants my embrace.
Dear Donald Hall, even before you
died, and you were so witty and kind,
you said you couldn't read much and
no longer trusted your judgement.
My first teacher, Howard Nemerov,
judged what John Ashbery wrote
not poetry and would not take
Mudfish with him to the grave.
It was too heavy to carry, he said.
>   *Jill. Yes. looking forward. Marie.*
I could hardly believe my eyes.

JOHN ASHBERY CELEBRATION ON ZOOM

When you're out of red
You're out of wine, John Ashbery said.

The shoulders of a virtuous woman
Are the last to go, Balzac said.

Probably no one here will vote for
Trump, Stephen Paul Miller said,

But you never know.

A SERPENT'S TOOTH

I woke up crying in recovery.
                  A nurse asked, What's wrong?
Is it the pain? No, my daughter, I cried.
We weren't speaking because she
                  likes Maxine Waters and I like
Fox News.
                            Later the same nurse
unidentifiable behind her mask, asked
Are you feeling better? Yes, I answered,
it stopped hurting.
I mean emotionally, she said.

My daughter
sharper than a surgeon's saw, calls
me a racist,
                my firstborn, my proxy,
my cure.

She texts: But you call me
brain-washed
a self-hating Jew
uninformed

Good list! I text back
    (though I don't remember self-hating Jew).

Our last years
shaky as an outdoor table at Caffe
Reggio's on MacDougal Street
where I order Rome by Night and she
Iced Mocha with Whipped Cream.

A FINE CONFUSION

A lawn about the shoulders thrown
into a fine confusion.
—Robert Herrick

We were in his bedroom, all three of us, you,
me, and the dog. I had been thinking about
his walk-in closet with tweeds, flannels, silks
in full display (my clothes lynched on hangers,
inaccessible in mangling darkness—my leather
jacket torn!). The light was off and we sat in the
dark. Then the light was turned on and he was
there at the table and I held my breath because
he didn't look our way but I could hardly believe
he didn't notice us, or hear our breathing. Or
the light had been on and now was off. I was
too embarrassed to know, like when I was a
small child lying to my mother about a dress
with a sheer organdy pinafore that I said I
had removed at school and carefully folded
so that it wouldn't get wrinkled during rehearsal
but was actually sewn on! The maid ironing
saw me standing perplexed in the closet
and said, "I never saw no one thinking so hard."
When I woke up next to you, and the dog
emerged from under the bed to lick our toes
and you started to tell me your dream, I was
distracted remembering mine, and the day
darkened as if I had done something wrong.

GHOSTS

(After a painting by Charles Yuen, on the cover of *Mudfish* 22)

We are walking on our own graves
and lying down at night
above our buried
selves

And everybody dies
and nobody dies
because
we are only here for a moment
anyway

As an old boyfriend said
as I showed him the door
everything has to end
sometime

And time is a gift
like Nessus' shirt
that takes off your skin
when you unbutton it

But all the ghosts
remember you
with a pinch of your cheek
and a kiss on your lips

SAAB

We were old when we met
but this morning when you left
like an astronaut in your old Saab
blue-eyed and clean-shaven
to go to your abandoned house
in Weston, Connecticut
—and I had had a bad night
because my leg couldn't find a
place to land under the wine-dark
comforter and I was also afraid
to fly to your grand-daughter's
bat mitzvah as an invalid with a
cane—you were miraculously
young. But I had a burst of energy
as you were leaving and wanted
to go with you but there was no
time and the dog couldn't go out
there by himself because of coyotes
and ticks, though afterwards
I collapsed in exhaustion and you
called from the car that was
still not air-conditioned—
where both our dogs used to sit
in the backseat like a married couple—
and I couldn't hear because

you had taken out your hearing aids
and the wind was blowing your words
out the window, "I'm exhausted," I said.
And when you answered, "You've been
exhausted for twelve years," I was
a bride beside you in my white
nightgown, your voice, a tin can
scraping along the highway to the end.

KNEE REPLACEMENT

I like the doctor. Everyone who
enters his operating room
must wear two pairs of gloves
one over the other to avoid infection.
I think of Gladys at Bellevue
who got one infection after another
and three years later still can't walk.
The infection came from her own skin
they told her. They tell me to wash
with antimicrobial soap from the knee
down and not to shave for five days
in case of an open wound. I begged for
a razor after open heart surgery
to shave my legs because you were
driving me home, and they gave me
one without a blade. I flooded the room
which was a shower without a stall
trying to be desirable whereas they
thought I might try to slash my wrists.
You drove each dawn from Connecticut
to be there early enough to wake me.
"How long have you known each other?"
a nurse asked. "Four months," I said.
"That's long enough," she answered.
I was happy, it was my honeymoon.

Now I have to get re-tested for Covid
even though I've had both shots. A long
Uber ride to a white tent on 100th St.
It will cost a hundred dollars there and back.
I'll hold your hand tightly while you talk in
Spanish to the driver along the silver river
on the FDR Drive, confident that we'll have
at least another hundred years together.

DEATH AND THE MAIDEN

for Paul Wuensche

I was high on Marinol (two pills like pearls
3x a day) and giggling a lot when we went to see
Lucian Freud in a townhouse—the leg sticking out
from under the bed—who had an affair with his own
daughter. And death was a mile away.
                                    When I got home
once from the hospital, the paintings on the walls
lit up like an illuminated manuscript
including my painting in the guest bathroom
of you in a park in Barnes painting a tree
("You should be painting *her*," a passerby had said).

You had not written for years. You wanted to paint
and when you weren't painting, to think about painting.
Nadia in a bathtub, the bathroom window panes looking out
on a garden teeming with exotic blooms. Now you write
every day from your magic armchair, poems
that arrive on my cell phone as I wake like white
mummified roses in a mirrored box delivered by a skeleton,
and in another month or two I will give up
my flowered cane and walk on waves to visit you.

KIMONO WITH YOUNG GIRL SLEEVES

Reading her poems, after Sharon Olds' sold-
out reading with Edward Hirsch, I make noises
as she did, when I could not see her—moans
of grief, or pleasure—listening blindly in the third
room of Lillian Vernon Creative Writing House
with her voice piped in to bundled listeners.
We had met once long before on B'way and 86th
in a store for kids who were going to camp,
and she had written a poem about eating
Moo Shoo Pork with her husband, safe
among nametapes and sheets and shiny trunks.
When I got to the front of the townhouse
her hair was white and dotted with barrettes.
Later, I re-read *Stags Leap*, backwards,
in my kimono with young girl sleeves
that hang down to the floor (that came with
the warning: *do not go near the stove*),
following her lines as if I'd written them
with my own suffering which is reborn in my
old heart as if I were again naked and young,
stepping on thin ice and hearing the crack.

THE MASCARA BRUSH

At eighty, you know you are old
but you don't believe it.

After Don died, Aunt Bebe had a
dream that she beat him up! "Oh
did I give it to him good!" she said.

At the cemetery when Aunt Harriet
was being buried, everyone
was remembering how
on her wedding day she dropped
the mascara brush on her white
gown.

I wear what the Jews
sorting through the clothes
of the naked called
The Shiny,
my dead relatives'
frivolous gold.

LAME VILLANELLE

You would not believe the pain I'm in.
I won't tell anyone I'm hooked on oxycodone.
Not from my kneecap made of titanium

But from old muscles trying to be young again.
Your Uncle Gustav lost his leg in the war.
You would not believe the pain I'm in.

In the basement we found his silver-handled cane
With which he wrote "Pig" in the dust on your floor.
I needed a cane for my knee made of titanium.

I won't tell anyone I'm hooked on oxycodone.
He was a Jew who fought in the first World War.
You would not believe the pain I'm in.

You write the word "Pig" on my skin
With your nose. And cut the last small pill into four,
Just for my kneecap made of titanium.

Your mother's list for summer camp written in German,
It's hard to tell if I'm hooked anymore.
You would not believe the pain I'm in,
But not from my kneecap made of titanium.

IN JULY, DEATH COMES TO FRANKLIN STEET

Hands, you are old.
You shake measuring salt.
Veins are blue sirens *en route*
To a synagogue in Park Slope
That warn the end is near.
Dear heart, beat your drum.
The days parade on. Andrew,
The building manager, is dead.
Thursday, he rode his bike, went
Home, had chest pains and died.
Shareholders weep. On the sidewalk
Outside my window, the widowed
Building sheds tears.

STILL LIFE

Ah Sunflower, alone in a vase
bent slightly over the pottery edge
in the dimly lit living room

On a large glass table with two bronze
mermaids for its base, nubile
children with raised bronze arms

Not quite reaching the glass oval
that floats above them like a placid sky,
the surface of the placid ocean

With two cabbage salt shakers on it
because the lady of the house likes
cabbage, and a ceramic French pepper mill

You are half the length that you were
before a man with a scissors came
to lengthen your golden life

— and put your clipped stem out on the hard
concrete to wait for the garbage truck.
Inside, we dine until death comes.

DIVORCE

"Dating is hard work," he said. "She was
very nice but I wasn't attracted to her
at all. I have a type. Tall and thin. She was
tall but I guess not thin enough."
"You'll find someone you're attracted to,"
I said. "I'm dating someone I'm attracted to,"
he answered. "But I can only see her
every other weekend and she may not think
that's enough."
                                    "Why don't you do
what Amanda does and have her visit
on the weekend when the children are there?"
"Because that would be bad for the children."
"How can you be so disciplined?"
                                                "Because
I love my children more than I love myself."

This was an indictment. I was a bad mother.

He was driving home from halfway between
where the woman lived and where he lived.
The phone rang in the car and I held on.
When I was jilted by a famous artist
—*I craved no other nor no better man*—
I met a poor handsome artist who my

73

children hated and he lived with us.

My son was back in an instant. "Who was that?"
I asked. "The woman from dinner," he said
grimly. I tried to say something about looks,
that in the end other things mattered more.
"Especially when you're old." Then there was
a second call.
                    "I have to take this, Mom."
He hung up, energized. I hoped it was the woman
he wanted, who might want more.

OLDER WOMEN

He came into the examining room
and his hair was silvery grey — I was
a little shocked because to me
he was so young. He was wearing a
mask and I was used to seeing only
his eyes. It was surreal like a dream
in which you're not sure who it is.

You're not sure who you are either.
Are you really 82? he asked. You
asked me that the first time too, I said.

Later he said, Do you know the
song, *Older Women?* When it came
on the radio when I was a kid — it
was just country music — I used to
go wild. My sister was a concert
pianist. Do you know the Mannes
School? She went there.

I was in the dark, unmusical.

Suddenly I cried, I knew the owners!
They came to my house! Their son
was a critic who read my novel,

Stoned, and said, what are these
asterisks between paragraphs—is
that where you took a break to smoke
pot?
      But he was already out the door,
our fifteen minutes were up.

That night I dreamed I was let off
someplace. I didn't know whether
I was on 82nd Street or 62nd.
My eyes couldn't read the sign.
I wanted to walk downtown—but
the streets were dark in the
pandemic and there was
no one to ask the right direction.

Later I found the song and played it
on YouTube: *Older Women make
beautiful lovers. . .Older women know
how to please a man.* I burst out laughing,
exploding with pleasure—as if he and I had met
on Jewel Avenue before the invention of
time—but Jack was watching and I
covered my face with my hand.

HAND-PAINTED SCENES

My garish purple kimono
from Old Japan
teaches me
nothing lasts
The white silk lining
frayed and torn
beyond repair
I've lived in it
and now
lying in my coffin
in repose
with the long
lavish sleeves
folded over my heart
I remember my
young days
a Geisha
on her knees
hand-painted scenes
like Charlotte Solomon
depicting window
after picture window
of her life
covered with German
words
in an enormous book

until she tried to marry
in Nice and the Nazis
found her

Nothing is lost, my mother
said, I want you to know that
Jill
All my teachers
teaching me
revelations continue
after you leave
the classroom
like learning
in an article in
The New Yorker
Howard Nemerov
was sleeping
with Diane Arbus, his
sister
when he called me
after I graduated
wanting to come over
late at night
in New York
and I was elated
and said no
maybe days
before his sister
committed
suicide

Secrets are toxic,
my mother wrote
Stink bombs
under Burkas
explode
in Afghanistan
Our demented President
secretly
looking at his watch
as each coffin is unloaded
Nothing is secret

JANE CAMPION

I remembered Harvey Keitel's
buttocks in *The Piano* which I saw
last night for the second time.
He lives in my neighborhood,
we have grown old together.
We say hello or nod and smile
when we pass on Hudson Street
or Greenwich. A beautiful
movie, more beautiful years
later, its passion rivals the story
of my own long life. I didn't
remember that Anna Paquin the
daughter betrayed the mother
she got along with so well
which is important to the plot
and can in your own life
wound like a hatchet.
This Labor Day weekend Jane
Campion is in Venice at the
Biennale for her new movie
The Power of the Dog
and maybe Harvey Keitel is too,
or else I might run into him and
blurt out that that isolated image

of the beauty of his buttocks
was burned into my memory.
Or tell him to tell Jane Campion
how great I think she is, making
The Piano with every mute
scene breathtakingly speaking
its ivory words like piano keys.
And how I also remember, and
always will, the row of sisters in
An Angel at My Table holding
on to each other and turning over
and over in bed like waves in
the ocean, like my lover and I
in my small room in my small
queen size bed.

MY KIMONO

has turned into
Dr. Dentons
I wore it proudly
answering the
door
I didn't mind
gold threads
unravelling
among its rich
purple design
pale green leaves
—as a child I
always plucked a
leaf from a tree
and clutched it
in my hand
for hours—
with sprays of
white lines
against the silk
background
and wild
wide-petaled

Japanese daisies
in many colors
my backside
completely
exposed
I can only
hope
the messenger
serving me papers
was distracted
by the small dog
like a blossom
barking
and failed to
notice

THE CONTRACT

On her deathbed,
Jane Kenyon had 8 poems
accepted by *The New Yorker*.
Not even a smile on her pretty
face. I painted her portrait
from a b&w photo Don Hall
sent. He didn't like the painting.
She was on top of a hill, Bald
Mountain, with her collie, Gus.
"I'm glad that Gus got in there,"
he wrote. "The trouble is, she
isn't pretty, and she was
pretty as hell!" he said. "That's
all right, she doesn't have to be
pretty," he added, always kind,
always a gentleman. Shannon
Hamman a poet who fell off his
roof, said in a poem every line
has to have a surprise in it.
His death was his surprise.
You canceling our contract is
my October surprise. You
were taking over *Mudfish* to
preserve my legacy. Instead
you set a bear trap and I
got trapped in it.

JENNY

I dreamed my black diamond
stud fell down your bathroom
sink—a deep hole like a belly
button—I was putting on
earrings and I fumbled
paralyzed expecting you
to help while for once
you just stood there
watching it disappear
though you were so
quick and young

BUTTER KNIVES

I hate putting silver back in its case
but I don't mind spending days, hours,
weeks laying a word in its tight velvet
slot. As I will be placed in a coffin one
day—I still can't believe it. Forks,
knives, different sizes of spoons.
I hate eating breakfast with a dinner
knife. I was glad when the dish-
washer chopped off two long blades,
like Anne Boleyn's head put at her feet.
I brought them to Steve M. the family
jeweler. I still want to call Renate and
hear her sweet high-pitched voice. I feel
guilty that I haven't visited my mother
and don't know where my father is
staying, now that they're dead. I am a pall
bearer with a bad rotator cuff, and
conscience. The living, forgotten, can
fend for themselves. My dark sister
four years younger is nowhere to be
found. Trees send nutrients to each
other underground. I send my poor
love to you in gnarled words that
travel slowly, thoughtfully, past
buried socks, grievances, and grudges.

RELAY

I tried to pass the torch
and I got burned by it.

The runner who was to
take it off my hands

set me afire, my hair
my Olympian outfit.

My bare arm turned
purple instantly

the last leg of the
journey.

ADAM

Getting back
what I didn't want
but spent
my whole life
begetting

getting back
at those
who took it
from me hard-
heartedly

like Eve
driven
from the garden

like Jean Seberg
found naked in her
car under a
blanket because of
her dead baby

I feel sorry for
Adam my pro bono
lawyer
who has a hard
job

A BUSHEL AND A PECK

In the kitchen you
Brush the crack
In my ass
And ripe apples
Spill
From a tree
That grows suddenly
In the back
Yard.

It was how I learned
To type in Junior
High: *I love you*
A bushel and a peck
—Fingers tap-dancing
Home from school—
A bushel and a peck
And a hug around the
Neck.

I am like the girl in a novel
I read a review of once in *The*
Book Review Section who
Had an orgasm every time
Her husband touched her

Even on the elbow.
I was so jealous
I couldn't read the novel

Or remember the title
Or the author's name
So I could never
Find the book again
(I remember I was disappointed
It was written by a
Man). You touch my knee
And I am
Young again.

A RUSSIAN FAIRYTALE

The 15-story building a lace
Antimacassar, its armchair
Blown away with the children
On my lap, turning the
Pages,
While I read to them.

DIFFERENT LINE BREAKS

for Daisy

A painting fell off the wall
and Jack put it back
horizontally. A nude and dog.
It looked better. You were
a curator. I was excited.
"It's about anal intercourse,"
I said, to be shocking.

You needed a ladder.
I asked you to get it
from the pantry
yourself. I was barefoot.
Then I felt bad.
Just standing there
in the kitchen, I fell.
I hit my head. My coccyx

cracked. My arm!
My arm!
I cried.

At breakfast a pink lily
you brought stares me
in the face,

the wet stamens like
paint, the fluted petals
floating
docked sailboats, yachts

I climb on deck, one
petal
torn
that will never grow back.
What is your favorite
flower? you asked.
You have seen men
wearing pearls.

WEEKEND GETAWAY

Peonies make you believe in God
Getting up early
Like peeking under the skirt of night
This is my life
A jumble of moments
A cortège
Headlights on on the new old car
In daylight
Driving to our own funeral
Behind my lids
Rhododendron blossoms like global warming
Scarlet and red
One leg
Sticking out from under the bed
Of my undoing
Sunbathing on the deck
Like Susanna among the elders
Like Susanna
Painting my breasts with sunscreen
While you watch from inside
Sitting at the kitchen table
Compiling expenses to offset our ruin

MARVIN

We must meet in front of
The office building
Where deer preside

Wild rabbis at an open grave

Your first cousin
Buried on his birthday
At 75

Will you be at my funeral
Or will I be at yours

Your cousin Bea in a wheelchair
Mum like Ezra Pound
In the Jewish Cemetery

I missed my sister
Seeing Queen Elizabeth on
The balcony on TV

                    Then the rabbi

Slashes the widow's blouse
The suits and shirts of the sons
With a box cutter

My eyes the well
Where Rebecca slaked the
Thirst of a stranger

The children and grandchildren
Recite in Hebrew
From a worn book

I am an illiterate member
Of the tribe

HIS PAINTING

Hearing aids on the glass table two shivering grey mice

Batteries fallen on the rug

His painting on my wall

Of green elders

Peering at an old

Susanna

Nude reading on the splintering deck against remembered trees

THEY WHO ONE ANOTHER KEEP ALIVE

Holding hands in our sleep
2 L-shaped hockey sticks
Wrapped in goose down
In July
In AC
Keeping warm on thick ice
The dog who bites you
Today on
Your birthday over a plastic
Pen cap
You attempt to retrieve
From his mouth
Is a blizzard-white featherbed

Leaning on my hip with his elbow

PAST LIFE

I barged into his space
Uninvited and was admitted
To my surprise and I was glad
To be there and see him from a
Distance because it still felt
Intimate but when I left he was
Already gone, and all the time
I was there all I did was worry
About where I could have
Been for all those hours
To tell you when I got home.

HELLO, BARRY

After the estate sale, coming back
To the pillaged house, a voice says
"Hello, Barry." Haunted, we chase it
From room to room. The clock radio
Is gone, the toaster oven, all the plates
Except the Limoges in the living room.
I have to pee before I cook, you say.
We are both on diuretics. Pierogies in
A small Iron pan. I hear them sizzle
As I read. We sit on two folding chairs,
Decorator wood with the tag still
On. $125 for set. Every unsold item
Has a price. On the floor outside
The bathroom—I leave the door half
Open for the dog—the head of a
Woman you painted averts her eyes.
Crenshaw melon for dessert.
Naked In bed, the dog between us,
I still like you, though 12 years have
Not left us blameless of blemishes.
We admire the dog. *You look so
Beautiful lying there,* you tell him.
In the morning, the smoke clears.
Above the staircase to the second floor,
A siren in her cigarette voice
lures, *Low
Battery.*

YOU NEED A BOOK

for Stephen Ackerman

The same way you earn
a dog's trust, you need
a book not single
poems
to make a reader
fall in love

I met a man at an MLA meeting
where I went to get a job
who was married
and from Michigan
I was wearing a leather
briefcase and he said
If only we could consummate
our fantasies

I met a man who was 86
on a train the same age
as my father when he died
and I was 56 the same age
as his wife and he was a Vet
for the Kentucky Derby he
wrote me once though he
couldn't write

I kept the book you sent me
and the small bubble wrap
package it came in on my
lap so the dog I held
wouldn't scratch my legs
in the car

but if I had bled
it would have been our marriage

ITTAI WEINRYB

Bits of magic
In the universe
That hardly matter
A boy I loved
So much history
Between us
I discover is
Your teacher
Father of your
Medieval knowledge
Meeting you
In the low-ceilinged
Gallery of life
I'm landlord of
Makes me want
To live forever

BAMBU PAPER

I see a woman at a medieval window
smoking a joint, the smoke curling
its arms out over Central Park

while a man rides away on a horse
down the yellow stripes over the tar
highway to Lakewood, New Jersey.

Why is she wasting her life over this
highwayman? Why is she robbing
herself? Why has her daughter twice

forgotten her key to the castle and
taken the bus to Lakewood so late that
she had to wait till six in the morning

at the Port Authority Bus Terminal for
the first bus, just to get the key from her
mother, and take the return bus home?

Why does her daughter hate her?
Why did she leave to live with her
father and then come home to betray her?

BAD FLOWERS

Once my daughter who was eight or six
bought me tall orange chrysanthemums
when John Ashbery was coming to dinner.
"I don't like them," I said. They were too tall, too
flamboyant; the chili I'd serve wouldn't live up to them.
("I had chili for lunch," John Ashbery said, adding
"this is much better, I have to admit.") I was
dry-mouthed. I smoked pot. I was a bad mother.
I adored her, except when my son was born,
then I loved only him. Now they are both coming
for Thanksgiving with their children. Turkey, stuffing,
pies, mashed potatoes, string beans, exhaustion,
grandchildren I hardly know because they live in
Georgia, where their mother said, "You mean, Matt
being in the hospital trumps Christmas?" Divorced.
Three children going between two houses, their mother
eating alone in her room or doting on the new boyfriend.
"Never leave the house on the day of a dinner party,"
my mother warned.
                         Now I am giving away
all my books. I know I will never read them again
and the ones I haven't read, have had their chance
for all these years. I can lie down on the empty
shelves and pillow my head on pure emptiness.
My father built these bookcases for his law office.

My son was tall enough to reach high shelves,
he noted, when Matt worked for him one summer.
I am on the phone with my father who is dead.
He was hurt when my mother went to Reno
behind his back and divorced him. I made it worse.
"It was the first decision she didn't regret," I told him.

When my mother died in the middle of the night
I left a Frank Stella pastel drawing he did for her
signed, *For Pearly, love, Frank,* on the hospital wall.
There was one like it at the Downtown Whitney
Inaugural Show valued at a humble million.
"If you really want to be my woman," he'd said,
"you'd let the hair grow under your arms." And
he said, "I have to sit around all day thinking of
things to say to you that I don't want to say."
Our mutual friend was dying of leukemia;
he was sleeping with both of us. I went away
on my Guggenheim. She died. When I got back
he was engaged to someone else. "I love you,
I love you, I love you," he mocked, "and what did it mean?"
My mother called him 'Perky' because he was an addict
and bought her Percodan. He put five hundred dollars
in my jeans' pocket. I watched him put a pill in his mouth.
I take Gabapentin for hot flashes. Like Sir Thomas Cranmer,
I burn at the stake. No one else my age still has them.

Like Frank– I swallow without water.

My next boyfriend
pulled his empty pockets out like rabbit's ears. He hated
my children and they hated him. My mother said
about my father, "I don't want *him* to be the man at my
funeral, I don't want *him* to be the man there."
The man I want at my funeral is a widower
whose wife ran marathons, his house a tag sale,
fifty medals on ribbons, a wall of wooden plaques.
She died of baby powder. Her souvenir mug I drink
coffee from, is called 'Grandma's Marathon.' My dog
was in love with his, and for a year, when his dog died,
mourned terribly. Death has married us, a skeleton
under a chuppah. I put my arm around him from
behind and press my body naked against his,
our two graves, waiting, far apart.

SPEECH AFTER SILENCE

I baked some cookies, you should
have one, I say on the couch;
a strange remark to make
at the gathering to celebrate
the passing of a friend. *Oh, I will*,
she threatens in a sultry voice,
the lost daughter, a trojan horse,
a coconut full of fentanyl at the
open border between life and death.

ELLIPSIS

Man Ray's model Kiki with boy hips I always wanted
naked on the cover of my first novel, raises her arms
over her head seductively, dead now, as is Carin
Goldberg who put her there and won a prize for it.
I failed to thank her for thirty years. Then we met.
I kissed her the moment I saw her, forgetting Covid.
She swims every day to keep sane with a brain tumor
under her bathing cap she knows is fatal—her dog
swam with her. I had not been in a pool for years.
"You look eleven," she said. "You're so relaxed."
She got out of the pool to talk to me. Her 'blind date.'
Reclining on a beach chair, one arm over her head,
I watched her compress her whole life into a few
sentences—her mother dead at 40 in a parking lot
surrounded by Amway boxes; telling her son in California,
'I'm alright if you're alright.' "I don't mind my lost career
or my hair, but I mind leaving him, and Jim," she said.
She still swims brilliantly, hugging the edge with an
even stroke, level-headed and alive in the blue pool
of sky her architect husband James Biber built.

FALLING

I would never leave you, even though I sleep
naked, and you sleep in a t-shirt always cold
We sit at breakfast like a Bonnard. I am wearing
my winter kimono, the dog like a cream puff
licking our feet. I remember that Nabokov said
he had to stay home with the muse and not attend
his award ceremony, which I didn't understand
when I was young. We had just driven to
New Brunswick to see the retrospective of Komar
and Melamid in the Zimmerli Museum. I fell
for the third time in a row, going down the stairs,
holding onto the railing and your hand.
The first time, I fractured my eye socket.
They said an eye muscle might be trapped
in the bone fragments that could leave me blind.
There was a painting by Alex Melamid after he split
with Vitaly called "Modigliani with Eggs," that I
stood in front of puzzled for several minutes.
I was the nude covered with broken egg shells.
Then the next morning scooping egg shells
out of the kitchen sink suddenly I remembered
the dream I thought was a clip I had seen
on television. To his surprise, a man fell
into a hole and, unexpectedly, it was his
grave, and others shoveled dirt on top of him.

RED DOT

A red dot over my crotch meaning *sold*,
I am married at last to John Donne in his shroud.
Did you know he sat for his portrait hooded and
gaunt for three weeks before he died? Poor man.
The nameless artist who painted him, dead too.
Your father went to synagogue in his shroud on
Yom Kippur and was married in it to show eternal
love. In graduate school they told us being a poet
was divine. You would live forever. Not die
poor and unknown. This is my love poem to you.
I want to be buried with the first two lines.

OLD COUPLE

Every day I get worse at belly
Dancing.

Dear God, I pray, let me not
                                                     fall
On my face today.

I am unable to serve
Guests in my own backyard,

Hanging onto chairs and
The long slender trunk

Of the Japanese Maple
Petrified, as if aboard a

Sailboat, about to pitch
Overboard.

Your love Is no ballast.

But on the street
Holding hands

The laity murmur, 'Young love.'

INSTAGRAM

My grandson like a Greek god
Posts: First Tat.
Is that him? I'm not sure.
His hair an explosion of black
Curls
On an urn containing my ashes.

FOR JOYCE

I have always disliked
Tattoos
But seeing them rain
Down your slender arms
Inexplicably
In a Chinese dance
Of fans and umbrellas
Crossed fingers and
Landscapes
In colorless colors
Enchants

JENNY, AGAIN

How did I go from girl
To 80 something?

This weekend I met
Old men on benches.

I told one I lost my daughter;
She wasn't speaking to me.

You can go on, he said; another
Said: You don't need her.

Oh, reason not the need.
I drink from the pottery mug

She gave me. You shop in my house
She said. I lost my prescription

Sunglasses under her bed
When she had a tummy tuck

And couldn't bend down
To look for them.

I was wearing them later
When I fell and broke

My eye socket and lying down
Saw double. When I had a knee

Replacement she didn't come
To the hospital. I had to go

Through that not having you,
I said. (This was over politics.)

You had me, she said, and I
Was comforted. But now

It is *irreparable* she told a friend,
Who asked, Maybe you'll make up?

No, she said, and shook her head.

GEORGE SEGAL

My sins, like a wedding gown floating down the Hudson,
The night drowning my dreams except one or two,
A woman complaining to me, Jill, your dog bit me three times,
And then looking for the dog in a flood that had covered the car
And now was green earth.
                    In the morning, I try to add up
Who I am: if you want to know who you are, your mother told you,
Look at your friends. Evelyn in a car with the daughter of my ex-
Husband's parents' friends. The daughter says to her, Sorry, Ev,
I'm going to let go of the steering wheel now. I picture the white-
Haired couple sitting on the white sofa in Boston like the white
Sculptures of George Segal in the park in the Village near the subway
Sitting on benches or standing in groups that I pass going to have my
Hair done, or in the past to make love with the artist you say blew
Smoke up my ass.
                    Evelyn had another friend who announced the date
Of her own suicide. Something to look forward to, jot in your day planner.
The sin of my marriage. The sin of adultery to blot it out. The sin
Of not believing I will die when the cemeteries are so ripe with graves,
Abby, Terry, Renate, my parents, that I gravely place white stones upon.

GOLAN HEIGHTS

Every ten years your number comes up.
I got my Guggenheim in 1974, so my number
Is 4. The first time in 2004 and then again
In 2014 I was invited to a Guggenheim
Party. New Guggenheims were given out
And old fellows were invited to attend.
Joyce Carol Oates was there with her
Husband. My former husband had
Written our budget for going to London
Which Is how I found out I had won. I told
Jonathan Baumbach in our shared office
At Brooklyn College that my husband
Embarrassingly had listed toilet paper
As an expense and Jonathan said that means
You've won. "If they ask you for a budget
You've won." It was my first time applying.
"I applied eleven times and never got it,"
He said. I felt sorry for him when Noah
Baumbach vilified him in his film; then my
Daughter in her novel did the same thing
To me. A man died that night of a heart attack.
He was taken away quietly in an ambulance.
I asked but never learned the details.
The views are astounding. From
Edward Hirsch's office you can see

All the tall buildings of heaven on earth,
You are at the height of immortals
Wearing olive branches in their hair.
You try to network; I'm not good at it.
A handsome poet who was a doctor
From Palestine came from California
Where he lived now to get his award.
"You're Jewish, aren't you?" he said.
"Yes," I said. "I knew it," he remarked
With a hatred like a drawn sword
I had never experienced before.
"They took my family's house away."
This was before Hamas beheaded
Babies, burned them in their cribs,
Bound whole hugging families with
Steel and burned them alive, before
Women were raped then tortured
On command: *do anything you want*
And I saw one on television over and
Over pulled by the hair her sweat
Pants stained with blood on her behind
As she was shoved into a car to be killed.
The butchery of 2023. In 2024 I will
Go back again, to those spectacular heights
If the building is still standing, if I am.

SURROUNDED BY FRIENDS WAVING HAMAS FLAGS

The sink is full of dishes because the dishwasher
Flooded the kitchen, the repairman didn't come
From 8 to 12. Chicken Little, the sky is falling, the
Sky is falling. The President is chicken. Winken,
Blinken, and Nod. Some kitchen towels look like
Keffiyeh. You must wear one to be safe.

DANCING ON OUR OWN GRAVES

We bought a mattress together
the dog was with us
we had to drive to Brooklyn
and find the place
he met us on the street
it was like a palace
he had bought years back
full of back rooms and balconies
stairs the dog tried to climb
to explore

then we lay down on beds
together soft then hard
harder and harder
until we lay on the hardest
mattress of all
and after one night of bad
dreams—the holocaust/
the holocaust
to come—
we lay on a silver platter

our shoes worn out
in the morning

IF ONLY TO GO WARM WERE GORGEOUS

Inside the shower wall a shiny copper pipe,
the tiles from Sri Lanka are pearly white

Some sky blue tiles blue sky, a small
window blocked by a toppling tower

of ancient towels, the showerhead with
mysterious powers, the four walls closing in

so that I can never fall or fail to dream
in the hot water and inspiring steam

John Ashbery said he never minded being
interrupted by a phone call in the middle of a

poem like Kamilo interrupted after making a hole
in the ceiling when he went to get his tools

and found his truck window smashed
and his plumbing tools gone

HARD WORK

I have a serious job to do.
It's my turn.
"Always leave them laughing,"
my mother said, before her one trip
to Israel
taking out life insurance at the airport
from a big coin-operated machine.
"Dying is hard work," your Uncle Gustav said
with his wooden leg and his silver-handled cane.
It's nothing
I ever thought about before.
"You're 84," Deborah Axelrod said. "You'd better
make up."
Even making the bed, I fell. There was my painting
of my daughter taking up the whole wall
or I would have reached for it
to save myself.
"You have this heaviness in your heart,"
Sasha said. "You don't want to live with that."
George said, "Go. Apologize. Bring flowers."
When I wrote about my dying mother
who wore cobwebs on her legs
for pantyhose and sneakers she had bought
tied together by their laces
in a supermarket, she said, "I have made up
my mind, I will love this novel."
I will go to her book launch and try.

BEFORE AND AFTER

Before, I had my hand on her arm
and she had her hand on his
shoulder (her other son wasn't there)

—she was my Rock of Gibraltar

After, I have a knife in my back
and she has red nail polish on
that drips my blood on her book

THE RAPE TREE

My bloomers on a low branch,
I cross the border
to old age where I never thought I'd
be. I look around. Short women with canes
walk in pairs. I have a knife in my back.
My daughter betrayed me.
I will never forget her fat
satisfaction at my expense.
She that herself has slivered
and disbranched from her material sap*
—I am the sap!—is fringed with glory.

In the past I wore short shorts
with fishnet pantyhose and rang his bell
at intermission; he was in bed
with another woman. "I would be embarrassed
to be seen with you," he said. He loved my
best friend and I didn't know it
until she died and two years later
he married someone else.
"You think about someone for two years,"
he said. I hurt for forty years.
Mere child's play compared to this.

Blood from my heart flows down
along my ribs. "You have a problem
no copyright can solve," a lawyer said.
Who can I leave my mother's Sweet Pea
China to, registered to the Queen?
Who will wear her pins and necklaces, her
ropes of real pearls that bore her name?
Or walk on the deck her teak coffin is made of?
Outside my door, the sidewalk is waiting
to crush me in its concrete arms and kiss me
with its mica lips.

*King Lear, IV 2 35

WHAT IF THIS PRESENT WERE THE WORLD'S LAST NIGHT?

What if this were my last day?
I'd go to the dog store and buy Vermeer
a treat, I'd sleep late and get a ticket
on the windshield of our car, I'd buy one tube of paint
and write a message on my chest
in ultramarine violet

ACKNOWLEDGEMENTS

Golan Heights; Surrounded by Friends Waving Hamas Flags ***TABLET MAGAZINE –NOVEMBER 10TH, 2023***; Saab; Jenny, Again; A Serpent's Tooth; A Resemblance; Dancing On Our Own Graves ***MUDFISH 24***; Aubade; The Contract; Jenny; Judge Wanted ***MUDFISH 23***; Thou Preparest a Table Before Me; Jenny Kissed Me; Oh, My Dear Franz; Light Years; O My America ***MUDFISH 22***; A Dog Is Where We Put Our Soul; I Am Young; And Summer's Lease Hath All Too Short a Date (as "Summer's Lease"); John Singer Sargent; Late August, Franklin Street ***MUDFISH 21***

With special thanks to Joyce (Chunyu) Wang, who taught us how to use InDesign for the first time, and for her creativity and lightening speed. And to Elodie Hollant for her dedication and help. And to all the members of the Mudfish Writing Workshop. My deepest thanks also to the poets, writers, and artists who were kind enough to read and appraise this book.

ABOUT THE AUTHOR

Photograph by Laura Hetzel

Jill Hoffman's first book of poems, *Mink Coat,* was published by Holt, Rinehart and Winston in 1973. Her first novel, *Jilted,* was published by Simon & Schuster in 1993. She founded Box Turtle Press in 1983 and has since published 44 books: 24 issues of *Mudfish,* starting with *Mudfish 1984 and* 20 issues of Mudfish Individual Poet Series. *Kimono with Young Girl Sleeves* is Mudfish Individual Poet Series #20. Before that, Box Turtle Press published her collection *black diaries* (poems) in 2000 and *The Gates of Pearl* (a book-length poem) in 2018. In 2023, a second novel, *Stoned,* was published (Mudfish Fiction Series 1). She is also a painter and has painted the covers for many of these books.

Hoffman has a BA from Bennington, a Master's degree from Columbia and a Ph.D. from Cornell. She received a Guggenheim Fellowship in 1974 to 1975. She has taught at Columbia University, Brooklyn College, Bard, The University of North Carolina, The New School, and other institutions. Presently she teaches a Mudfish Writing Workshop on Zoom from her Tribeca, New York studio.

ADVANCE PRAISE FOR *KIMONO WITH YOUNG GIRL SLEEVES*

Kimono with Young Girl Sleeves is a beautifully alluring title, and the poems that follow surprise and delight with their candor and with the skillful irony that permits the poet to translate autobiography into poetry.

David Lehman, *One Hundred Autobiographies* / Series Editor Best American Poetry

Decades ago, in her first book of poems, *Mink Coat*, Jill Hoffman wrote "In the open book of my life/I can be seen at all hours." In *Kimono with Young Girl Sleeves*, she has written the new open book of her life, employing in her art the intimacy of diarist, the precision of a knife-thrower, the eye of a painter and, above all, the ravishing gifts of a true lyric poet, to give us the story and the stories of her life. In *Mink Coat*, she wrote, prophetically: "I long to see myself as an old old/ woman." In *Kimono with Young Girl Sleeves*, with courage and candor, she gives us the haunting and enthralling poems of a woman still passionate, still vividly alive. She gives us "My old funny life/Of heartbreak/ And ecstasy."

Stephen Ackerman, *Late Life* (Gerard Cable Award)

Jill Hoffman is a phoenix rising from the ashes with each new book she publishes. And yet, there is a particular poignancy and emotional urgency in her most recent collection, *Kimono with Young Girl Sleeves*. In her poem "Ghosts" after a painting on the cover of *Mudfish 22*, the literary journal she has edited and published for decades, Hoffman writes, "We are walking on our own graves / and lying down at night / above our buried / selves / And everybody dies / and nobody dies / because / we are only here for a moment / anyway." Her poems demonstrate that she is happy, she is funny, she is smart and open to whatever comes her way, and she is willing to fight like a warrior for another day, and the chance to rise from the ashes like a beautiful and majestic bird in her colorful and spectacular *Kimono with Young Girl Sleeves*.

Dell Lemmon, *Single Woman / Are You Somebody I Should Know?*

Kimono with Young Girl Sleeves is the compelling new collection by poet Jill Hoffman, writing at the height of her powers to survey a life spent in the New York art and literary worlds. Bringing a painter's eye for the vivid image to vignettes of the ordinary and everyday, Hoffman spins them into thrillingly sublime effect. Set against the upheaval of Covid, these poems speak to love and estrangement, hope and heartbreak, all under the illuminating shadows of advancing age and mortality.

Richard Mott, *Poet and Environmentalist*

Jill Hoffman's poems have a compulsion to throw themselves into tumultuous life. Their flamboyance and pleasures cannot be divorced from the anxieties of family life or friendship. And the poems keep on returning asking for more. Her devotion to dogs—and their own perilous lives—cannot be separated from friendships, lovers and children. No one is left off the hook here. There is a courage to this experiencing of life and facing up to its contradictory needs. The poems evince themselves in the risk of life. A courage of writing exemplified in such poems as "Lame Villanelle," "Relay," and "Ellipsis."

Richard Fein, *Losing It / Dear Yiddish*

The poems from Jill Hoffman's new book *Kimono with Young Girl Sleeves* talk about difficult subjects – aging, death, the loss of loved ones. They are written by an aging woman, but they do it with honesty and the audacity of youth. The fearlessness of her work makes it relevant and very much alive.

Anna Halberstadt, *Vilnius Diary*

It is such a pleasure to be invited once again into the floating world of Jill Hoffman's imagination. This is the best kind of poetry: generous, passionate, and brave. There are no taboos here. Hoffman enters the darkest corners of experience and finds beauty everywhere. These are not just exquisite poems: they are fierce testaments to the power of poetry to reconcile us to life.

Paul Wuensche, *Painter and Poet*

From the opening poem about first love, to being bloodied and wounded by those who are supposed to love you, Jill Hoffman's new book of poetry *Kimono with YOUNG Girl Sleeves*, throws us into a fire of heartache and sadness yet exuberance for pressing on. She paints in ultramarine violet, belly dances, cares for pets and partners, and is bound to her ancestry. In this intimate, intense and revealing book, Hoffman shares the dialect of rage while illustrating the resilience of women. I don't only love these poems, I am grateful for this collection being in the world.

Paul Schaeffer, *The Cruelties of Brooklyn*

The poems in Jill Hoffman's *Kimono with Young Girl Sleeves* chronicle her long life as a poet and a painter. Her voice is modest, sometimes full of sadness, and essential. I admire the restraint and perspective found in her spare language. The poems celebrate a creative life tempered by loss and longing, discovery and delight, and unexpected moments of pleasure.

Rodger Moody, *Self-Portrait / Sixteen Sevenlings*

Jill Hoffman's poems have an honesty that teeters on the edge of revelation and then swipes left before too much family blood is spilled, and from the flesh wounds memories emerge whose lethal points are wrapped in olive leaves. Hoffman namechecks various contemporaries with praise both robust and faint, more generous nevertheless than most of her fellow scriveners in the insular world of New York poets. This lively collection from her octogenarian period is a muscular, tender and singular contribution to an overcrowded field.

Max Blagg, *Late Start for Mardi Gras*

Kimono with Young Girl Sleeves is a tour-de-force, striking at the heart of what it means to be alive; you'll find yourself laughing and crying as Hoffman mediates on art, aging, love, and loss. Like Vermeer, or any master of interior life, she beautifully illuminates the moments that make a life whole.

Ross Barkan, *Glass Century*

It's very comforting to live in the world of Jill Hoffman's poems. These are full of poets out and about in the world, always talking and writing. The poems have such tender affection for efforts at honesty. Poets' thoughts, on paper and in life, mingle with one's own, providing some inkling—in the back of a mind, as one buys one's groceries—of what life might actually be like.

Karin Roffman, *The Songs We Know Best: John Ashbery's Early Life*

Other Publications by Box Turtle Press

MUDFISH INDIVIDUAL POET SERIES

#1 *Dementia Pugilistica*, David Lawrence

#2 *black diaries*, Jill Hoffman

#3 *Too Too Flesh*, Doug Dorph

#4 *Skunk Cabbage*, Harry Waitzman

#5 Unavailable

#6 *marbles*, Mary du Passage

#7 Unavailable

#8 *Rending the Garment*, Willa Schneberg

#9 *Vilnius Diary*, Anna Halberstadt

#10 *Single Woman*, Dell Lemmon

#11 *The Gates of Pearl*, Jill Hoffman

#12 *Notes for a Love Poem*, Mary du Passage

#13 *Conversations with the Horizon*, E.J. Evans

14 *Are You Somebody I Should Know?*, Dell Lemmon

#15 *Losing It*, Richard Fein

#16 Unavailable

#17 *The Cruelties of Brooklyn*, Paul Schaeffer

#18 *Dear Yiddish*, Richard Fein

#19 *Death, Please Wait*, Rochelle Jewell Shapiro

MUDFISH FICTION SERIES

#1 *Stoned*, Jill Hoffman

Coming soon:

#2 *Rabbits Are Strange, When You Are a Stranger,* Alexander Iskin

#3 *Topless,* Jill Hoffman

#4 *Arnold2,* Robert Steward

Order at our website: www.mudfish.org

Praise for Stoned

In Jill Hoffman's irresistible *Stoned*, the poet Maud Diamond not only indulges in reefer madness in her Beresford bathroom, but takes a much younger live-in lover, a handsome Russian (would-be-famous) artist, to the horror of her precocious children. An explosive triangle, by turns hilarious and heart-breaking, brilliantly drawn with outsized characters worthy of Dickens, lavish imagery, and impeccable comedic timing. Hoffman has written a book so poignant and pleasurable, like a Crème Brûlée for the eyes, you'll read it again and again. And yet for all its seeming decadence there is a purity here like a fawn running into the water.

Stephanie Emily Dickinson, author of *Razor Wire Wilderness; Harlow/Smith Postcards: Icons in Black and White*

18th Mudfish Poetry Prize Winner to receive $1200.
Judge **Vijay Seshadri**, 2014 Pulitzer Prize winner,
author of *3 Sections*. Guidelines for submissions
on our website: www.mudfish.org

SUBMIT YOUR OWN INDIVIDUAL POETRY VOLUME OR NOVEL

Inquire: mudfishmag@aol.com or 212.219.9278

Box Turtle Press, Inc.
184 Franklin Street
New York, New York 10013